PET CARE

FISH

BY KATHRYN STEVENS

The Child's World®

Published by The Child's World®
1980 Lookout Drive • Mankato, MN 56003-1705
800-599-READ • www.childsworld.com

Acknowledgments
The Child's World®: Mary Berendes, Publishing Director
The Design Lab: Design
Michael Miller: Editing
Sarah Miller: Editing

Photo Credits
© 101cats/iStockphoto.com: 13; aluxum/iStockphoto.com: 3, 22 (platy);
c-foto/iStockphoto.com: 3 (net), 10, 20, 23; Foto_by_M/iStockphoto.
com: 8; GlobalP/iStockphoto.com: 21; HirkophotoiStockphoto.com:
4-5; JohannesK/iStockphoto.com: 5, 22 (blue); Kathleen Petelinsek: 12,
cover, 2, 14, 20 (food); Kristof Degreef/Dreamstime.com: 7; Mangroove/
Dreamstime.com: 16; Olias32/Dreamstime.com: 9; Peter Pavel
Losevsky/Dreamstime.com: 18; Pomorski/Dreamstime.com: 15; Petar
Lazovic/Dreamstime.com: 11; saavedramarcelo/iStockphoto.com: 17;
TatjanaRittner/iStockphoto.com: 5 (yellow), 24; Vangert/Shutterstock.com:
cover, 1; wimammoth/Shutterstock.com: back cover, cover, 2, 6 (betta)

ISBN: 9781631437328
LCCN: 2014959754

Printed in the United States of America
Mankato, MN
July, 2015
PA02262

NOTE TO PARENTS AND EDUCATORS

This Pet Care series is written for children who want to be part of the pet experience but are too young to be in charge of pets without adult supervision. These books are intended to provide a kid-friendly supplement to more detailed information adults need to know about choosing and caring for different types of pets. Adults can help youngsters learn how to live happily with the animals in their lives and, with adults' help and supervision, can grow into responsible animal caretakers later on.

CONTENTS

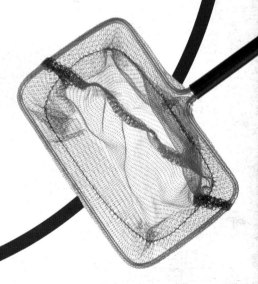

FISH AS PETS

Fish make interesting pets! People love to see them up close. They enjoy their bright, flashy colors. Even little babies like to watch fish swim. Some kinds of fish are easy to keep as pets. Others need special care.

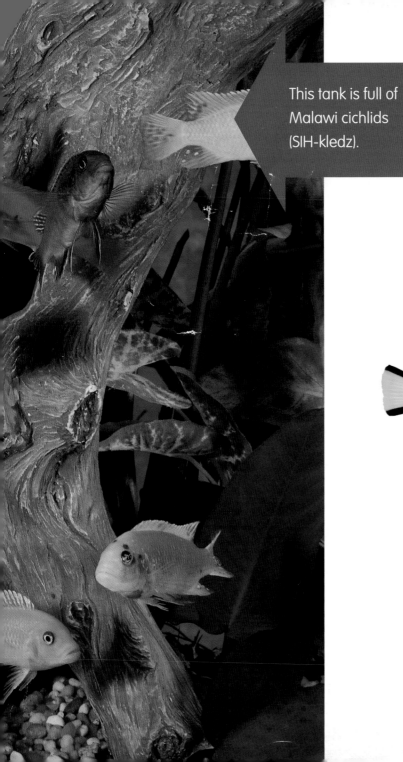

This tank is full of Malawi cichlids (SIH-kledz).

Tangs are fish that live in salty water. There are many types. This blue tang and yellow tang look very different from each other!

Some kinds of fish live together well. Others do not. They might fight or even eat each other. Size is something to think about, too. Many fish start out small but keep getting bigger. They need a big enough place to live.

Betta (BAY-tuh) fish like this one are also called Siamese fighting fish. Male bettas cannot be kept together, or they will fight.

People often keep goldfish as pets. But many goldfish can grow too big for small fish tanks.

This aquarium has lots of hiding places for fish.

A NICE HOME

Pet fish live in clear tanks called **aquariums**. The fish should have plenty of room to swim. They like places to hide, too. Rocks make great hiding places. So do underwater plants. **Gravel** covers the bottom of the aquarium. It comes in different colors.

Some aquarium plants are real. Others are made of plastic.

CLEAN WATER

Fish spend their whole lives under water. They even breathe under water. Air bubbling through the water helps them breathe. A **filter** helps keep the water clean. Sometimes aquariums need more careful cleaning.

People with pet fish learn how to keep the aquarium clean.

A bubbler puts air into the tank for these cichlids.

Some pet fish live in salt water. It is salty like the sea. But most pet fish live in freshwater. It is not salty. Some fish need cold water. Others need warmer water. Water from the tap can make fish ill. Special pills or drops make tap water safer. So does letting it sit for a few days.

Pet stores sell special drops for fish tanks. It makes the water safer for fish.

TAP WATER CONDITIONER™

AQUARIUM DECHLORINATOR

Removes chlorine and breaks the chloramine bond

WATER CONDITIONERS

This aquarium has saltwater fish. They come in all shapes, sizes, and colors.

GOOD FOOD

Pet fish eat special fish foods. Different fish eat different kinds of food. Feeding fish is easy. You just sprinkle the food on top of the water. They only need a little at a time. Too much food makes the water dirty.

Fish food often comes in thin flakes.

GOLDFISH FLAKES

CLEAR WATER FORMULA

NET WT .42 OZ (12g)

This goldfish is eating food flakes that are floating on top of the water.

GOOD HEALTH

Some pet fish live for only two or three years. Others can live for 20! Taking good care of them helps. Careful feeding is important. So is keeping the aquarium clean. Sometimes fish get sick anyway. Animal doctors, or **vets**, can often help. So can pet stores.

A cover keeps the fish from jumping out of the tank. It keeps cats away, too!

Plecos (PLEE-kohz) are great to have in a fish tank. They eat gunk that grows on the glass. They are a fun way to keep the tank clean!

LOVING CARE

Fish are not cuddly like some pets. But they are fun to watch! A nice, clean aquarium is bright and beautiful. The fish in it will stay healthy. And people will enjoy seeing them swim in their underwater world.

This aquarium is clean and bright. Watching its colorful fish is lots of fun!

NEEDS AND DANGERS

NEEDS:

- the right-sized aquarium
- a water filter
- bubbling air
- hiding places
- the right food
- aquarium cleaning

DANGERS:

- no aquarium top
- dirty water
- no air in the water
- too much food
- soap or cleaners
- heat or cold
- too much sunlight
- the wrong fish living together

FUN FACTS

BODIES:
Fishes' body shapes move easily through the water.

EYES:
Fish do not have eyelids. They never close their eyes, even when they sleep.

SCALES:
A fish's body is covered with thin scales.

GILLS:
Fish breathe by moving water through their gills.

SIZE:
Some goldfish grow to be 1 foot (30 centimeters) long!

FINS:
Fish use their fins to move and steer in the water.

GLOSSARY

aquariums (uh-KWAYR-ee-ums) Aquariums are clear tanks where animals can live.

filter (FIL-tur) A fish-tank filter cleans dirt and food out of the water.

gravel (GRA-vul) Gravel for fish tanks is made up of small, round stones.

vets (VETS) Vets are doctors who take care of animals. "Vet" is short for "veterinarian" (vet-rih-NAYR-ee-un).

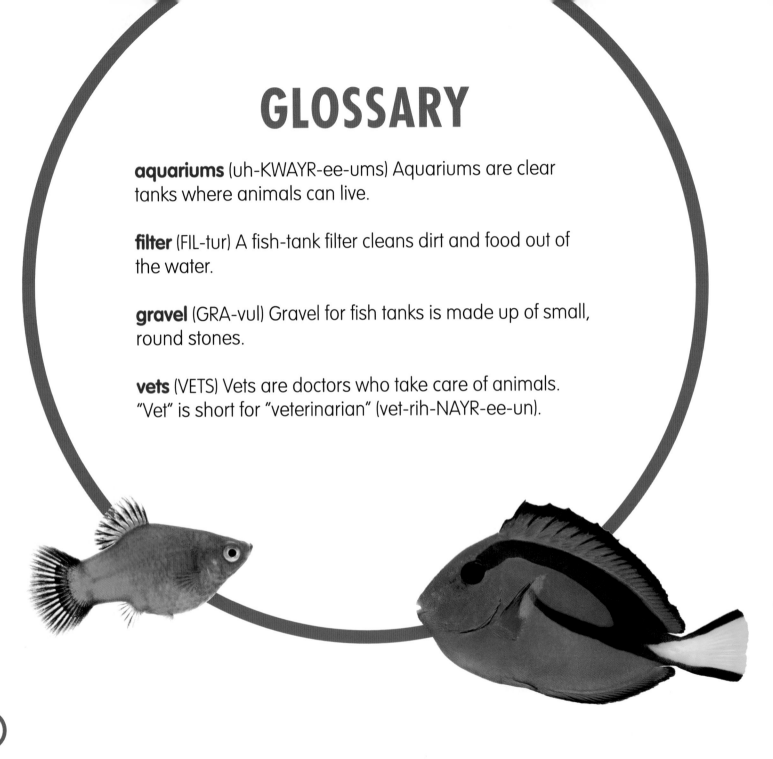

TO FIND OUT MORE

BOOKS:

Algarra, Alejandro. *Let's Take Care of Our New Fish.* Hauppauge, NY: Barron's, 2008.

Ganeri, Anita. *Goldie's Guide to Caring for Your Goldfish.* Chicago, IL: Heinemann Library, 2013.

Macaulay, Kelley, and Bobbie Kalman. *Goldfish.* New York, NY: Crabtree, 2005.

VIDEO/DVD:

Paws, Claws, Feathers & Fins: A Kid's Guide to Happy, Healthy Pets. Goldhil Learning Series (Video 1993, DVD 2005).

WEB SITES:

Visit our Web page for lots of links about pet care:
www.childsworld.com/links

Note to parents, teachers, and librarians: We routinely verify our Web links to make sure they are safe, active sites—so encourage your readers to check them out!

INDEX

ABOUT THE AUTHOR

Kathryn Stevens has authored and edited many books for young readers, including books on animals ranging from grizzly bears to fleas. She's a lifelong pet lover and currently cares for a big, huggable pet-therapy dog named Fudge.